Young Orville and Wilbur Wright

First to Fly

A Troll First-Start® Biography

by Andrew Woods
illustrated by Ellen Beier

Troll Associates

Library of Congress Cataloging-in-Publication Data

Woods, Andrew.
   Young Orville and Wilbur Wright: first to fly / by Andrew Woods;
illustrated by Ellen Beier.
     p.   cm.—(First-start biographies)
   Summary: A simple biography of the brothers who launched the air
age in 1903 when their flying machine stayed in the air for twelve
seconds.
   ISBN 0-8167-2542-X (lib. bdg.)   ISBN 0-8167-2543-8 (pbk.)
   1. Wright, Orville, 1871-1948—Juvenile literature. 2. Wright,
Wilbur, 1867-1912—Juvenile literature. 3. Aeronautics—United
States—Biography—Juvenile literature. [1. Wright, Orville,
1871-1948. 2. Wright, Wilbur, 1867-1912. 3. Aeronautics—
Biography.] I. Beier, Ellen, ill. II. Title.
TL540.W7W66 1992
629.13 '0092 '2—dc20
[B]   91-26479

Wilbur and Orville Wright were
brothers. They invented the first
motor-powered airplane.

Wilbur was born in 1867. Four years later, Orville was born. They grew up in Ohio and Iowa with their brothers, sister, and parents.

From the time they were little, Wilbur
and Orville were best friends. They loved
to build toys and machines together.

Their mother liked to make things, too. Once, she could not find a sled big enough for both boys. So she took wood and metal from an old stove and made one!

The Wright home was full of books.
In those days, there was no TV or
radio. In the evenings, the family
read out loud to each other from
books and newspapers.

In 1878, Mr. Wright gave Wilbur and Orville a gift they never forgot. It was a toy flying machine made of cork, bamboo, and paper. Its motor was a rubber band.

The boys named their new toy
"the Bat." They played with it
all the time.

Wilbur and Orville played with their toy so much that it broke! So they made another, larger Bat. It flew for a second—then crashed.

Wilbur and Orville had lots of fun together. They swam and played baseball and ice hockey.

The boys worked, too. When Orville
was only ten years old, he made kites
and sold them.

Orville also worked as a paper boy.
And he collected scrap metal and sold
it to junkyards.

Orville used the money he earned
to buy parts to build a special tool.

Wilbur and Orville used the tool to help build a beautiful new front porch for their house.

Their neighbors liked the new porch.
Soon the brothers were building things
for other families in town.

When Orville was a teenager, he started a printing company with his friend Ed. When Ed got tired of the job, Wilbur took his place.

Wilbur and Orville even built their own printing press. They used scrap metal and wood—and the press worked!

Soon the brothers started their own paper, the *West Side News*. It was a big success.

In 1892, Orville and Wilbur opened
a bicycle shop.

The brothers loved building newer and
faster bikes. They even made a special
bicycle—a bike that two people could
ride at the same time!

But Wilbur and Orville still dreamed
of flying. Together they planned their
own flying machine.

Over the years, they made and
flew many gliders, which are
planes without motors. Then
they began to build a new kind
of plane. This plane had a motor.

On December 17, 1903, their airplane
was ready. Orville took off from a
runway in Kitty Hawk, North
Carolina. The plane rolled along the
ground—then soared into the air!

Standing on the ground and watching
his brother, Wilbur cheered. Their
dream had finally come true!

Orville and Wilbur kept on building airplanes. Each one was better than the one before it. Each one flew higher and longer.

After Wilbur died in 1912,
Orville kept making airplanes.
But he never forgot his brother.

"We always worked together,"
Orville said before he died in 1948.
"We did our *best* work together."